*Ventriloquism – the art or practice of speaking or producing sounds in such a manner that the voice appears to proceed from some person or object other than the speaker…* (OED).

*I am crucified with Christ: nevertheless I live; yet not I, but Christ liveth in me…* (Galatians 2:20).

# Ventriloquise

Ned Denny was born in London in 1975. His debut poetry collection, *Unearthly Toys: Poems & Masks*, was published by Carcanet in 2018 and awarded the Seamus Heaney Prize for Best First Collection the following year. *B (After Dante)*, a version of the *Divine Comedy*, appeared in 2021. This is his third book.

# Ventriloquise

## NED DENNY

CARCANET POETRY

First published in Great Britain in 2023 by
Carcanet
Alliance House, 30 Cross Street
Manchester, M 2  7 A Q
www.carcanet.co.uk

ISBN 978 1 80017 331 6

Book design by Andrew Latimer, Carcanet
Typesetting by LiteBook Prepress Services
Printed in Great Britain by SRP Ltd, Exeter, Devon

The publisher acknowledges financial
assistance from Arts Council England.

# Contents

## I. Mode of the Orphan/Time to Die

## II. Mode of the Flowers/Alive, Alive-O

Ventriloquise

*To use words but rarely*
    *is to be natural;*
        *abstaining from speech*

*marks him who is*
    *obeying the spontaneity*
        *of his nature (this*

*"was an old saying",*
    *notes the translator, "which*
        *Lao-tze found and adopted");*

*use words sparingly,*
    *and then all things*
        *will fall into place.*

\*

*The poet writes, as I*
    *think Cocteau has Orpheus*
        *say, yet he is not*

*a writer; lies talk loud*
    *but are weak, the truth*
        *seems weak but is strong;*

*the secret's revealed*
    *to the one who knows how*
        *to keep silent in song.*

# I

## Mode of the Orphan/Time to Die

# Breath-Manifester

Each bared morning is a fine time to die,
Leaving the town's ornate maze for the level
Expanse of those lit and flesh-eating fields, the
Clouds that turn like ghost machines, the antic
Tremendous woods where Pan's breath on your heart
Recharms a flame from its grey-furred ember.
I'll wear my belt blazoned with Alpha Centauri,
For luck, whilst you'll surely sport that Oxfam scarf
In whose puce stitch some crone has worked *G.I.*

*E.* (Glory To The Most High). Time to die, to be
Disturbed by the one re-re-repeated Word
Fanfared by each time-warping bird, each fierce leaf
Or pimped bud that is but love's newest halloo
Over the heads of the dead and alive, alive-O.
Laughing, you'll lurch and say or missay, "only kenning what's real
Saves us from terror… Wilhelm Reich". Wise words.

# Two Poems After Ronsard

## i) A Drinking Song

Let my wine be well chilled, so
it tastes more fresh than melted snow;
let Jeanne come, and bring along
her guitar to play a song:
we will surely dance, us three.
Let me see you, nubile Clare,
tresses coiled in that pretty
style the mad Italians wear.

Days are, as atoms, empty.
Tomorrow's where we'll never be.
Get here, boy, and fill this slim
beaker to the crystal brim.
Curse those sheep who toil in vain,
the doctors' murderous advice:
am I ever truly sane
until steeped in wine like ice?

## ii) Bouquet

I send you this bouquet, which my own
hands just culled from the marvellous bed;
if spring's not gathered tonight, I said,
tomorrow her beauty will have flown.

Let its light serve as a sermon then,
how your charms flourishing their fair May
shall soon be invested with frost-grey
and, bit by bit, become forgotten.

Time paces restlessly on, my sweet,
and yet it is not time's but *our* feet
that point to a house beneath the hill,

and the joy we are now free to choose
is something of which skulls have no news:
*O love, love me while you're lovely still.*

# Chattels (Civitas Dei)

I live deep in the city in a glorified
shed lined with old books and threadbare flying carpets
and unearthed bottles loved for an aqueous light
the striped or speckled stones I've chanced on here and there

black paintings I have slowly harried into life
a necklace made from a king cobra's vertebrae
a bowl resurrected from the grave of the sea
I have elected not to be a happy slave

plants that are all ears several postcards a silence
broken only by the rain's agile fingers and
the bailiff thundering on the door but there is
nothing here that wouldn't turn to ash in his hands

# Blaze

We say we are ready to be eaten by the music
yet have scant idea what that entails,

what fire those geometric petals conceal.
In need of advice, we turn to the dead:

their eyes are forests, they cannot speak.
This room begins to seem a temple

raised to a pixellated god,
to the warp and weft of that ultimate blaze.

Did we never imagine the light's envoys
would be our furnishings and our toys,

that a wild grin of insect glee
was waiting outside the dormitory?

Phantoms are urging us to panic
but the whole city's a sounding bell,

the mind's ancient everglades
flourishing at last.

# Equinox

In the bare jasmine
the sparrows' white-hot outbursts:
its first, scentless blooms.

\*

Crocuses appear,
as though a buried army
all lifted green spears.

\*

The soundless drama
of a bluetit's fits and starts
counsels vigilance.

\*

Spectres of the fields,
poplars flaunt their skeletons
beneath opened skies.

\*

What's that Kabir says?
When you wake, your own garden's
the true Benares.

\*

Those dark, silent trees
we allowed into our streets
were Trojan horses.

\*

Morning's floodlit clouds
imagine mountain ranges
where no man can stand.

\*

The Lord to Joseph:
*See, compare my green fingers*
*with your calloused hands.*

\*

Through undrawn curtains
comes the wordless jubilance
of feathered spirits.

\*

The ash is doglike:
its buds are little black claws,
its twigs silver shins.

\*

An ant creeps through grass,
a jet through the troposphere
(both through the garden).

\*

The sun's gold hammer
cracks the grey nut of winter.
Nothing new, they say.

# Arrest
*after Chénier*


When the death-cave of the dark abattoir
      Gapes wide for a bleating sheep,
The shepherds and dogs, the slow flock, the far
      Fields are unaware as sleep.
The children who loved his leaps on the green,
      And the rose-complexioned girls
That showered kisses on his face so clean,
      Daisy-chaining those white curls,
Shall now – without one tender thought – praise stew;
      Buried in this living hell,
I have, dumb brother, the same fate as you
      At oblivion's hotel.


Forgotten like me in a house of pain,
      Thousands more blonde sheep will be
Skewered from arsehole to recusant brain
      And served to "democracy".
What could my fellow thought-criminals do?
      Yes, lines passed through the black grille
Might salve my dry soul like an April dew…
      Would *gold* assuage they who kill?
But day's now a prison yard; you were right
      To choose life. Friends, stroll at ease,
Be unwilling to take this road in spite
      Of your vanished liberties;
Perhaps in innocent, ignorant years
      I turned my own heedless heart
From the sight of some naked beast in tears.
      Live, citizens, live; be *smart*.

## Florescens

The bent apple tree bears light in the sun,
*Inferno* and *Paradiso* in one.

# Found Poem (Deity or Sacred Puma)

A human face is depicted
on its tongue. The pendants

hanging from its ears
are in the form of ceremonial

knife-blades. The front and back
paws have rings. The body

is entirely covered
with repoussé work which

represents a double two-
headed serpent. This design

continues up to the end of the tail
and it has an extra plate of

metal jutting out of it,
forming a kind

of pocket into which the
faithful put coca.

# Three Songs for the Turning Year

*i) Rondeau*

Spring lays down her tattered cape
of cold wind and biting rain,
now arrays herself again
in sun's fair lace, love's landscape;
there is not one quiet beast, no
bird without its sweet argot:
*spring's laid down her tattered cape!*

Rivers, mountains and small streams
wear a livery that seems
made by goldsmiths' cunning art;
all's apparelled in the heart.

Spring lays down her tattered cape.

*ii) Lament*

Grieve, grieve for the falling leaves; they
go to become another May.

New greens unfurl in empty places;
where grey age shook, a baby's face is;
on rouged cheeks see the teardrops' traces.

Grieve for the falling men; we burn
with autumn fire and won't return.

Life reascends and shines in flowers,
a light that is and is not ours;
winds rise and down white blossom showers.


*iii) Wake*

Autumn moons chill, spring's flowers yearn,
summers have storms, winters snow;
revert to the way of unconcern,
for the one wealth man knows is now.

# Night

Wherever the sun peers,
she is not there.

A forest on the move,
her dark frontier

steals round the earth
swifter than our drowned cries.

What can we say
that does not make light of her,

this silence that stalks us,
this jet-black, still

and always breaking wave?

\*

Yews as tall as mountains
and grey as ghosts

loom along her border,
a rushing veil

beyond which darts the bird
whose note can kill,

the snake whose bite is song.
She is the night

without words that we will
have to live through.

Look, her scouts already camp
by each loud bloom.

## Opium & Death

*after Heine*


They're almost identical twins, these two,
though he's pale as the other's blackest brown
and more forbidding – nobler, you might say –
than this sticky one, chased with Earl Grey, who
warms with his dawning smile the mind's bleak town
and whose countenance turns night to day.

It's an embrace yet an opening too.
The youth's dream-scented and blood-bright crown,
alight on your brow, burns all pain away
so that just *being* is something to do,
immured in that untold, antique renown.
It doesn't last, though. You're in the sick-bay
until the graver brother sets his torch down:
*sleep is good, and a good death heals you,*
*but surely better never to have come this way.*

# Five Poems After Wang Wei

*i) Shrine*

Endeavouring to reach the mountain shrine, I
find myself astray on pathways in the sky.

Unearthly chimes sweep this primordial wood.
I'd follow that stream to its source, if I could.

Beside the grey iris of a lake, at dusk,
I sit and subdue my inner basilisk;

unseen the rasping of the crags and waters,
unheard the gelid light on the dark, ranked firs.

*ii) Garden God*

At the stone of your eyes the stroke of rain;
the great house shuttered and silent now;

you stand and observe the moss's green
until it has climbed and covered your brow.

*iii) Lines*

With age I get too lazy to write verse;
solitude is my ever-youthful wife.
I was a poet in a former life
and have been not one but several painters.

Unable to quit the habit of art,
I've worked and achieved a certain fame;
the world, that is, knows some lines and a name,
yet does not and will never know this heart.


*iv) Farewell*

"Dismount, take a drink for the road, my friend…
in any case, where are you rushing to?"
"I have seen the ruin of all my plans,
am retiring to the southern highlands".
"Farewell, then, I've no more questions for you".

Above us the white clouds flowed, without end.


*v) Returning From Songshan Mountain*

The clear river slides like a snake of glass,
licks grassy banks, burbling of that and this;
my horse and cart go at reverie's pace;
roosting birds peer from leafy balconies.

Desolate town, decrepit ferryman!
Sundown makes the forest one blaze of gold.
Far below your silence, high Songshan,
I come home and shut my door against the cold.

# Bycatch

Grace is like a strange fish that came in a batch
of tetras and catfish
from Paraguay or Surinam,

its absolute transparency
ghosted by a rainbow-flash
of colours of which no one knows the name.

## Mughal Shade

The intellectual trance,
disclosing and concealing,
cast by the geometric art
of this forbidden ceiling
keeps me frozen and apart
from the real stars' pealing,
wild, unmentionable dance.

# Fone World (Civitas Diaboli)
*after Lorca*


*i) Crossroad*

\A sullen wind,
a streetlight
and the blade is
in the heart.
The city vibrates
like a string
pulled tight,
it buzzes
like a horsefly.
Everywhere I go
I see the blade
in the heart.


*ii) Flick-knife*

The flick-knife
enters the heart
as the ploughshare
pierces the soil's night.

    *No.*
*Don't stick it into me.*
    *No.*

The flick-knife,
like a ray of black light,

sets the secret
caverns ablaze.

*No.*
*I have no money.*
*No.*

# Ithaca

Gelled suitors rev outside the harbour's
vape shops and several "Turkish barbers",
whilst on this craven island's shore
new brutes are beached; a silent war,
a realm awash with cheap cocaine;
legislation descends like rain.

# Song
*after Heine*

Who invented the clock, pray tell,
time's division, the ticking spell?
An ice-cold man that hated song,
who sat and thought the whole night long
and listened to the starved mice brawl
and beetles pacing in the wall.

Who invented the kiss? I'll tell:
a lovely mouth, you know full well,
that kissed and did not think at all;
it was in May, the wondrous call
of bird and bloom adorning earth,
the sun-god roaring golden mirth.

# Maker

I go to bed early and rise even earlier,
make a pot of coffee and sit in the dark and purr
or step into the garden and wonder what God meant
when He made night air so sweet and spread our starry tent.

# Heaven

*after Supervielle*


In the hourless forest
a mighty tree falls

branching light trembles
above its outstretched body

now search for your calls
the site of your nest

whilst there yet whispers
sky-high memory

# Clareaudience

How good to stalk in clear autumn among
The woods the jostling streams the nettled fields
A drop of the elixir on my tongue
In the light of which each beheld thing yields
To the sight's inner ear its inner being
The ghost that hid beneath a leafy veil
(Mind still damping the blaze the eyes are seeing
Though they ascend like the horns of a snail)

Nature is music when vision is clean
And *every sound that meets the ear is love*
White tiers of the spectral clouds above
Lichen's unearthly glow-in-the-dark green
And November's flesh is coloured glass
Lit by the voice that shines deep within its heart

# Blue Skies

Claude's last canvas, *Landscape with Ascanius
Shooting the Stag of Sylvia*. The moment
which started calamitous wars. A murder,
that of the stag with his strange, dark face
by a huge-limbed man in a metal hat
and his chattering friends and their drooling
hounds. Hunter and hunted
stand on opposite banks of a river,
the great bow tensed, the stag oddly poised
as if a sudden sound has turned his head,
but other than this faint
hint of infamy it is the same perennial scene
Claude always paints.
                A civilisation is on the wane,
and amongst the ruins of temples and libraries
some indestructibly delicate trees
are dancing into the sky, tasting the breeze
with their green and numberless tongues. The clouds
are another world, the distance has turned
a mountain blue, and the tiny sail of someone else's life
punctuates the far-off shore. Then a nearer shore
where the deep-flowing river mirrors the heavens
as though the earth contained a second sky,
and, moored in shadow, the precarious boat
that poets steer. That they steer into skies
that dawn in the mind. And the stag, whose ears are cocked
not at voices in tree-tops, not at bursts
of coarse laughter or a dog's harsh cries
but at the drums of incipient war,
and who might for all I know be Claude himself,
calmly looks the arrow in the eye.

# Double

On an ice-wrecked outcrop stands a lone pine –
asleep yet awake, half-hidden in snow
plump and light as the whitest of duvets –

who dreams of a palm beyond Palestine
and her frayed fronds stirred by a wind as slow
as the progress of these murderous days.

# On Reading *A Treatise of Civil Power*

Death-muttering scholar who has forgotten
how to dance; citer of the holly's flame-
pliant youth, its jagged age; battler through
England's desecrated ruins, trailing
the High Table's insolent crew:

*was neuere leef upon lynde lighter*
than when I flung these garlanded pages
in the air, turning back to Eden's ashiver
lingerers; better their green courtesies
than the stoop of a crabbed and over-civil tongue.

# To the Fates

*after Hölderlin*


Just grant me one summer, powerful fates,
    and a final autumn of lucid song,
        so that, sated with music's sweetness, this
        soul may wholeheartedly die.

A poet not wielding his sacred might
    in life shall find no quiet in Orcus,
        yet once I have said the holy words I
        came to say, spoken my art,

I'll welcome then the still realm of the shades…
    I will be at peace, although I must leave
        all singing and travel alone; having
        known the gods, I'll ask no more.

# Replying to Subprefect Zhang
*after Wang Wei*

*for Antony*


Wiser now, I value quiet;
turning inward, I've no plan

but to be a wildwood man;
cares no longer cloud my heart.

Cypress wind bares me for sleep,
hilltop moon strums my guitar;

you ask why things are as they are;
anglers croon, the river's deep.

# Opening the Mouth
*after Basavanna*


It can be done with the aid
of the adder's bite,

or maybe the appearance
of dark Nibiru

looming out of the mind's night
like an evil dream,

for they'll never breathe the truth
while they're nailed inside

the casket of affluence;
yet when misfortune,

rare magician, comes knocking,
then and only then

*O lord of the confluence*
they'll waken and sing.

# Dusk: An Antique Song

The costliest of sequels, springtime hits our screens

with its air of revolution, its artful scenes
shot with golden filters, a hormone-heavy breeze
playing over all who have flocked to the feelies.
It's in 3D, naturally, the budding Queen Anne's lace
so delicately real it seems to brush your face,
the flower-starred kilim upholstering the ground
woven of dew and light. And listen: there's the sound
the grass makes when it grows, the illusionist's call.
Suchlike special effects arouse the usual
dopes, Lynx-reeking blokes in flip-flops and pink v-necks,

girls whose arms and eager breasts raise the ghost of sex
and the odd scowling poet scribbling on his knee.
It is time to depart in droves for the country
and to bask in a pharmaceutical sunshine,
ignoring the tree's semaphore on the skyline
and the frail, grey-veined petals pasted to our soles:
time to give an airing to our synthetic souls,
to submerge the birds' dark and indifferent argot
in tweets and blent ringtones, a din that will go
pulsing out across several nearby star-systems.

Someone comes knocking, seven brisk taps. "*You* listen,"
a voice purrs, "you roach, you dreamer! Ah, let me kiss
your throat. I am the auteur, I fashioned all this!"
But I'm no greenhorn, I lock that vampire out;
I'm wise to his game, how he works to bring about
an order that is disorder, a prison whose wall
is the size of the sky and close as the eyeball;
I can see through the thickness of polished cement

on buildings and men's hearts, observing the torment
of those who murder love in order to survive;

I see the movements of the lost, their features alive
as tainted meat plucked from supermarket aisles;
I see the terror stowed away in full-sailed smiles,
sweet desire debased because innuendo sells
and the truly-riddling holy fool's cap and bells
nowhere worn; instead of men I see the shells of men,
role players, limping shadows, aged children;
and every home's a mental home, each office a ward
where the evening discharge is each slow day's reward.
And deeper still than this, my eyes penetrate

far into the earth as if it was an agate:
foundations, dungeons, subterranean cities
where thwarted joyance wages its atrocities.
I see endless tiers of corpses, larvae-white
with great astonished faces, all swaddled good and tight
and pale yellow scorpions moving over them
like pit crews attending to their thrumming cars; then,
yet deeper, cold-blooded watchers in black habits
and mewling children with the crimson eyes of rabbits
in cage after cage, the monstrous progeny

begat by pure reason upon biology;
these are the horrors that each May would conceal
with its post-production suites, its glossy festival.
I also see the widow lying on a grave
beneath her lover, softly rocking just above
the coffin where her husband's scritching goes unheard;
the antique, new-discovered song of the blackbird
plays once more; small flowers laugh with wondrous malice;
a darkness tightens on the nations like a vice.
At dusk I sense the cry of the fallen Sophia

whose body this world is, I scent the fire
in her flesh and the cut junk blooming through her veins.
I see the metal in her side, feel her birth-pains
in my own head and I scream as it delivers
not one but a whole tribe of gigantic figures:
the sons and daughters of the jungle of the mind.
Leaping up the current of the solar wind
they quickly gain the light, circling with their grinning dwarves
the sun's brilliant citadel and its crystal wharves;
the spheres' ecstatic music skips once then continues

(a glitch unremarked on by the evening news)
as they storm into the cool of God's roped-off lounge,
the walls pearl-clad, the brooding bassline loud
and seraphim shrieking like panicked VIPs
around a sleek and shaven figure smoking at his ease.
With owl-feathered arrow or narcotic dart
the angels are dispatched, save one who stands apart –
that bright, that lovely one – and mouths exalted phrases
even while the lord of the forest approaches.
I watch those two embrace, as death slips into light,

the universe resounds, and once more it is night.

# II

## Mode of the Flowers/Alive, Alive-O

# January

The moon a ghost of herself,
a disc of ragged cloud

through which drifts a blue
more felt than seen. Trees,

free of their heavy
pelt of leaves, poised like gods

in thousand-armed frenzies
(lightning shot from mud

to heaven, each flung twig
striking the sky

which is the silence inside
a vast, bare mind

where bird-faced figures peck
at yellowed scraps of sun).

# A Dam

The girl loves me.
We touch, we tell
so warily.

I love her. See,
without her's hell.
The girl loves me.

I hear dark seas
in her ear's shell
so warily

I try to speak,
to break their spell.
The girl loves me,

and when we meet
we tremble well.
So, wearing leaves,

we pace this field
in which we fell.
The girl loves me
so warily.

# Atlantis
*after Baudelaire*

My sister, my child,
consider the wild
joy of the voyage, just you and I;
to love at our ease,
to die beneath trees
that inscribe your dark name on the sky.
The pure countenance
of three suns' brilliance,
refracted through the star-dewed spheres,
has the mysterious
charm of your dangerous
eyes when they illuminate your tears.
*All is beauty and order there,*
*savage calm, melodious air.*

Our chamber must be
furnished entirely
with teak which bears an age's patina;
the rarest of blooms,
uttering perfumes,
can vie with the scent of Baltic amber,
and mirrored ceilings
will counterfeit things
undreamt of by the Assassins' sect;
each object shall speak
in the sly, oblique
language that is the soul's dialect.
*All is beauty and order there,*
*savage calm, melodious air.*

See, on the canal,
the drowsing vessel
whose inmost mood is to wander far...
know she has sailed
from the end of the world
to answer to your truest desire.
The skies' blue-and-gold
transfigures each field –
the concentric canals, the vast city –
with hyacinth tones,
then plunges the zones
of our universe in glory.
*All is beauty and order there,*
*savage calm, melodious air.*

# Minoan

Creatures of light, our planet-
eyes swell in our upturned skulls

beside the gaping plants
of another world entirely. In

thrall to the flow
of the sun's current, the bull

dips his horns,
is part of the dance.

*


Two skeletons – one of bone,
one of light.

This close to the sun
the mind's flesh melts,

bares the rapt shape
of spirit itself.

*


The labyrinth a holy tree,
earth's black thumbprint,

and beaked goats snapping
at light-fatted blooms

beneath a heaven
less sky than ocean.

\*

At our fingertips, the thistly bursts
of sea-urchins or stars.

In these translucent bellies,
more constellations swarm. Our secret

being this – that the light
sees right through us,

that we have no weight at all.

# Vigil

It is strange to wake in a sleeping nation.
There's no outer sound or motion
other than that of the rain's devotion;

the dog lies down in his desolation,
the pane creaks with the weight of an ocean.

All eyes on the blaze's ancient elation.

# Two Poems After Mallarmé

*i) Chink*

Those zeroes, foam, that clear line
echoes but a glass's rim
as, far away, there plunge slim
sirens into sea-blue wine;

we voyage, O my diverse
friends, I upright on the stern
whilst you, at the sharp prow, turn
brows to lightning, tides, winters.

A fine intoxication
compels me to raise this toast,
standing tall and with no fear,

a toast to whatsoever –
solitude, star, coral coast –
is worth our sail's white concern.

*ii) O*

The smoke rings I cannot blow
seem summations of my soul
one by one by one they roll
scattered with another O

their trembling grey bears witness
to incendiary art
keep your ashen mind apart
from the buried fire's red kiss

thus whole choirs of romance fly
up to lips unclean with sin
just exclude when you begin
so-called realism's lie

for with too defined meaning
poetry will never sing

# Reading
*after T'ao Ch'ien*


June. The meadow-grass has grown taller than the mind,
trees like green lions shimmy in the slightest wind.

There's no bird that does not sing of the golden age
of being here now; my cool grove is this cottage,

looking out at the black soil where I've lined up seed...
if I wasn't so alive I would sit and read.

What palace official dares my unrutted lane?
Seeing the honeysuckle, they turn back again.

I pour myself a glass of medicinal wine,
pluck the lettuce the dew anoints, feel more than fine.

It is easier to laugh, easier to dance,
knowing oneself a person of no importance.

A mischievous breeze comes soft-footed from the east,
bearing the most delicate of rains in its breast;

remembering the stories of old King Chou, I
hold earth and heaven in the crystal of my eye.

This is called "reading the book of hills and seas".
The man that such vistas bore will never be at ease.

# DMT (Omphalos)

You put your head into the hive
and nothing's quite the same again.
Our flesh is light, our flesh is wild,

we are not who we think we are.
We teem with undiscovered stars.

Nature winks through a veil of names.

# Psilocybin
*after Heine*

I saw the elves in the wood last night,
riding in the light of the moon;
I heard their little horns ring out,
their bony bells' portentous tune.

They spurred past me as swift as thought
on mice whose antlers shone like gold;
those steeds flew silently as swans,
wild swans that range the southern cold.

Their queen nodded as she went by,
nodded and smiled (I held my breath).
Did that strange smile mean my new love,
or did that smile betoken death?

# Two Zen Poems

*i)*

My occupation, day to day,
is merely that which comes along:
nothing labelled "right" or "wrong",
nothing grasped or pushed away.

No purple robe of buddhahood;
blue hills without one speck of dust;
mysterious power dwells in just
carrying water, chopping wood.

*ii)*

Seeking the truth through others' sight,
the Self diminishes its light;

now that I travel on alone
I see it shine from every stone.

It is but the ordinary
mind, transcending us entirely!

Understanding the Way like this,
one joins with thusness as it is.

# Realm

Sitting there throned in perfect stillness
with respiration's nameless riches

you breathe as though you drink cool water
body invulnerable as air

a shaken snowdome slowly settling
the unmoved mover the one true king

# June
*after Hugo*

In summer, when light's fled, narcotic scents
are poured out from ten thousand blooms; we doze
with shut eyes but ears which only half-close,
immured by sleep of a strange transparence.

Deep shadows and the stars subtler, less bright;
vague radiance tints that eternal hall,
and the sweet pale dawn, awaiting her call,
seems wandering low in the sky all night.

# Cubist Painting

The unplayable note of silence explodes the guitar,
autumnal fragments fluttering in air.
Our empty glasses shatter to accommodate the sky.

The parlour fills with soil-shades, clear pond-light

as a violin's scroll slowly turns to snail.
In the circle of this broken pipe, a red sun nests.
Earth, my executioner.

The god is near.

# Two Poems After Neruda

*i) Ocean*

Body lovelier than waves
salt laving the sea-line
and the bird whose feathers shine
heedless of all my graves


*ii) The Sea*

No blood yet one single being;

death or a rose, a sole caress;
the sea comes in to shape our ways,

grows branches, strikes alone, can sing

through man and creature, nights and days.
Its essence: fire, cold. Restlessness.

# Talisman

The spray of cypress
I once picked from the ground
whilst waiting for you

behind a dismal estate,
albeit not real
but figured in plastic

(I can't say why
this feels significant),
and which for a long time now

has been hooked over
a blutacked print
of Dürer's *Melencolia*.

# Lapis
*after Yves Bonnefoy*


So we'll pace the ruins of a fallen sky,
far horizons blossoming

like places within reach, the light as though alive.
A land of salamanders lying before us –

those fatal, long-sought fields –
you'll show me a stone

bright with death's presence.
The secret lamp that burns beneath our limbs,

illumines from below.

# Comedy

*i)*

Satan lords it in darkness. He's real evil.

*ii)*

Up towards a shady garden you will crawl.

*iii)*

Words can't express how all those lights made me feel.

# Full Moon in Lent

In blue, smoke-scented dusks
where light is dangerous,
streetlamps whose reds
are glassed-in sunsets

start their vigil, bowed
over pavements a light
rain has made fathomless.
At the terrace's end

a wooded hill,
a purple-brown ghost
that floats or looms
over these sullen

and regimented lairs.
Beyond the trees, a moon
as cool as marble
hangs unspeakable, yet

is touchable;
contrives a stillness,
can be weighed
in the palm of the eye.

In narrow gardens, fruit trees
startled by winter
then frozen mid-flinch
brood on the im-

possibility of leaves.
The rank grass stricken,
mud in its element.
Now darker light handles

the greyed potting shed,
possesses each stone
as the sky's black freight
is loaded by increments.

This window's thin as ice.
Inside, familiar
objects fade from view
for all the light-bulb's

imagined honey;
words grow strange,
litter white like rows of flies
yet my child's blue eyes

are bright with love.
I can imagine nothing
but seclusion's end.
Unearthings are not deaths.

*Oxford*
*March 2006*

# Two Deathbed Sonnets After Ronsard

*i)*

I'm no more now than a sack of old bones,
despoiled and uneasy, sapless, unmanned...
night's black-feathered arrow has pierced me, and
I daren't view my limbs for fear of my groans.

Those two great masters of the healer's art,
Apollo and his son, look on and sigh;
goodbye, fair light, dusk possesses my eye,
flesh must descend and be taken apart.

Beholding this husk, this sea-whitened shell,
the sleeping face where grim death seems to speak,
and stroking my brow and kissing my hair,

who would pace home without tears on his cheek?
Farewell, beloved companions, farewell,
I'm bound for the deep, I'll wait for you there.

*ii)*

We must leave our homes and our orchards, these
vessels and vases Love's makers engrave,
sing a last song in the mode of the brave
shore-haunting swan and its wild obsequies.

It's done, I've unwound my destiny's spool,
I've lived and bequeath a corpse and a name;
my breath now ascends to the stars, aflame,
far from this world where the wisest's a fool.

Sweet not to be born and sweet to return
to the silence one is, sweetest of all
to be new-made and to dwell with the Son –

discarding to swell and rot in the sun
the body that fortune kicked like a ball –
and as both man and deathless spirit burn.

# Black and White

Even hell has its
compensations – the
faintest trace of light
on some foul beast's maw,

just as heaven has
its terrors – the ghost
of a shadow cast
by an angel's jaw.

# Potsherds

*i)*

To mouth the word's honey, I take in my mouth the bee:

she will bear me to that centre-
stone, that hive of song,
the pine-cone, the aviary
where speech whirrs its [...] feathers, where none dare enter
but athletes of the drum and the universal gong:

death's wave this second
overwhelming me,
no longer life's crowning terror, the long-unreckoned...


*ii)*

Pursue the branching paths of silence...
... for ... minds of men are blind...
... ubiquitous hound [of the?] sky-eyed goddess,
I the clear prophet...

... her all-seeing hands
... silver antlers ... laughing
... sinuous ivy of the drums [...] rebegin...

eternal
...

*iii)*

War is sweet to "advisors", those
who fatten well from fields of dead,
yet a thing of horror and dread
for the man who knows its sorrows…

*iv)*

Slow as an unerring arrow, O glowing song…

*v)*

Happy are they who have seen the end, [poets] tending
the tendrilled garden of their cry.

# And the Matter of the Hour Is as a Twinkling of the Eye

*Dwell at peace in the high pavilions*
of light you saw in a beggar's face once
the sky-house with portholes like jackals' eyes
revolving toward the Antarctic ice
the voice at the same time paean and lament
heard by the heart if thought is silent
while they mewl and cringe in a pathless wood
taking good for evil, evil for good

I touched my lips with the glowing ember
my room became an electric chamber
and the bird whose song was the barest sound
most clearly expressed we were homeward bound
the day is a book that proclaims the Friend
the nights declare our origin and end
little barque little bark tempest-tossed
everyone is found when everything is lost

# Wild Child

*after Hugo*

Tomorrow at dawn, when the countryside whitens,
I shall leave; that you are expecting me I know;
I'll go through the forest, cross over the mountains;
I can endure this distance no longer, and so

I will pace as transfixed by my thoughts as the mad,
insensible of every sound, of every sight,
hands clasped behind my bent back, alone, unknown, sad,
travelling through a day that is shadowed like night;

I won't admire the sunset's catastrophic gold
or boats in the distance, sails round with desire,
and then when I arrive I shall place on your cold
tombstone a bouquet of holly and briar.

# Redpilled

The primordial man,
says the Tradition, was
"without caste", meaning that

all roles and ranks were yet
latent within him; so,
too, an awakened soul

and all the deities
who've descended to earth
to intervene in our

long dream. Similarly,
the Zen master Rinzai
refers to the Self as

"the man of the Way" and
"the true man of no rank",
his term *mu-ye* also

meaning "independent"
and, in a manner of
speaking, "having no clothes";

you must be or become
priest, warrior, peasant
and pariah in one.

# Twilight

Trees resume their stature
like labourers unbending,
like museum gods
that blink and stretch at night.
Their giant forms against the sky
are a kind of speech:
poised, dark, gentle.

The bamboos by the river
are wild, brooding greybeards
out of ancient sagas no one reads.
The crickets tune in to the infinite,
a bird-call plucks the silence.
It is all still here.

# Iron Age

*Secol si rinova;/torna giustizia...*

When the mind is bewitched by a marble in space
and the citizens wince at a naked face
and new strains of deceit are going around
and the dead demand to be more tightly bound
and they scramble nine jets on glimpsing a dove
and drive in the nails yet call it love
and cameras watch live Eden's knoll
and separation is the protocol
and it's bugs for you while they feast as they please
and Medusa smiles from a billion TVs
and the medicine's seeded with wasp-eyed death
and all you can trust is your own wild breath
and "disinformation" is cried at the Word
and they tell the biggest lie this chained world's heard
and commit the greatest fraud hell's ever seen
and claim the stricken tree is green

when a dragon is about to be crowned
and streets are empty save for the drowned
and the wolf has the lamb's best interest at heart
and the Israelites circle the poison dart
and you need your device to leave your zone
and the dimmed sun is white as a desert stone
and the hungry ghost of the moon descends
and the axle of the heavens bends
and the suited thieves slip through chinks in a rock
and the hands are frozen on every clock
and a black horse rides upon manback
and still you think you're not under attack

and they lock the night to keep us safe from the Lord
and at scheduled times the slaves applaud
and Death is getting desperate and iron old

a bird will sing *dawn wield your gold*

# Posthumous

To set out into that landscape emptied by rain,
the ghost-wood track past the castle; alone again,
together again, speechless prattler, wise man, fool,
the sole sound rain's tap on the hood of my cagoule;
not a thought to shackle me, not a word to blind me,
everything before me and everything behind me.

# Notes

*When he first published his* Odes, *Thomas Gray "was advised, even by his Friends" – as he later wrote – "to subjoin some few explanatory Notes: but had too much respect for the understanding of his Readers to take that liberty". Baudelaire drafted a manifesto-like preface to the second, expanded edition of* Les Fleurs du Mal, *yet at the last minute gave it up. "Faced with the devastating vanity and uselessness of explaining anything to anyone," he said in a letter to his mother, "I stopped short. Those who know me well will guess what I mean, and for those who can't or won't understand me, I'd only be piling up explanations in vain." The following are meant neither as explanations nor to pretend to an erudition I do not possess (Eliot speaks somewhere of the poet's "necessary receptivity and necessary laziness", to which I might add "necessary ignorance"), but as mere hints and pointers such as I myself would find interesting; having committed one indiscretion, that of publishing my poems, I may as well commit another.*

["To use words but rarely"] the first part juxtaposes three different translations of the opening of the twenty-third section of the *Tao Te Ching*, by D.C. Lau (Penguin, 1963), James Legge (Oxford, 1891) and Richard Wilhelm/H.G. Ostwald (Routledge & Kegan Paul, 1985) respectively; the end of the second part has its origin in a phrase attributed to Aeschylus by Maurice Blanchot in his essay The Paradox of Aytré (*The Work of Fire*, Stanford University Press, 1995).

[Breath-Manifester] "mind- (or "spirit-", "breath-") manifesting" is the literal meaning of the word psychedelic, coined by the psychiatrist Humphrey Osmond in a 1956 letter to Aldous Huxley. In the tarot deck the Fool may appear at the start or end of the Major Arcana and is either unnumbered or numbered 0, the numeral that is both emptiness and fullness, alpha and omega; one writer on the subject identifies him with "the Green Man, the harbinger of a new cycle of existence, the herald of new life and fresh beginnings" (*The Tarot* by Alfred Douglas, Penguin, 1972). The *Princeton Encyclopedia of Poetry and Poetics* (Macmillan, 1975) notes that "in ancient times mystical significance was attributed to acrostic compositions". "Kenning" implies an intuitive, bone-deep knowledge but is also, as a noun, "one of the periphrastic expressions used instead of the simple name of a thing, esp. in Old Norse poetry", of which the poem's title is an example.

[Chattels] this poem came about from the chance meeting of a red-lettered missive threatening to "levy distress upon [my] goods" and a poem by T'ao Ch'ien, the opening lines of which read – in Arthur Waley's translation – "I built my hut in a zone of human habitation,/Yet near me there sounds no noise of horse or coach./Would you know how that is possible?". The "glorified/shed" was part of a former Bermondsey metal box factory, and the inventory of goods taken from life (the "bowl resurrected from the grave of the sea" being an item from the Vung Tau cargo, auctioned at Christie's Amsterdam in 1992); the poem's 144-syllable form predates the stanzas of *B (After Dante)* by several years.

[Arrest] written by Chénier whilst incarcerated in the prison of Saint-Lazare in spring 1794, not long before his execution, and smuggled out on strips of paper hidden in a laundry basket; it seemed particularly apt when I made my version in the superficially idyllic, but in fact cowed and credulous, days of late March 2020.

[Equinox] the oral poet Kabir, whose work I discovered in Linda Hess and Sukhdev Singh's *The Bijak of Kabir*

(Motilal Banarsidass, Delhi, 1986) was born in the holy city of Varanasi (or Benares) around the beginning of the fifteenth century; his "absurd, paradoxical, crazy, impenetrable" and deliberately provocative statements have much in common with those of Zen.

[Found Poem] Source: *Peruvian Gold* (Arts Council, 1964).

[Three Songs For The Turning Year] adaptations of the famous rondeau by Charles d'Orléans (1394-1465) and lyrics by the Ming poet Qu Dajun (1630-1696) and the Zen master Wumen Huikai (1183-1260).

[Bycatch] "bycatch" refers to any fish unintentionally netted along with the target species; I am thinking of the relatively small-scale capture of tropical freshwater fish for the aquarium trade, where unknown species are still encountered, not the indiscriminate destruction of a vast array of marine life by industrial trawlers.

[Mughal Shade] the imperial tombs of Delhi, where this poem was written, circumvent the Muslim law against indoor burial by means of a painted representation of the heavens.

[Clareaudience] this poem is my penniless homage to the riches of John Clare's last, long-unpublished collection *The Midsummer Cushion* (Carcanet, 1990); the translucent quality of nature on misty autumn days is something I have often noticed or fancied ("as the eyes of Lyncaeus were said to see through the earth," says Emerson in his essay The Poet, "so the poet turns the world to glass, and shows us all things in their right series and procession"); the weird yellow-green of tree lichen recalls the daytime hue of the luminous stars that children once stuck to their bedroom ceilings.

[Blue Skies] the painting hangs in the Ashmolean Museum in Oxford, where I first saw it in 2005 or 2006; the apparent anachronism of classical ruins in a pre-Roman landscape suggests (perhaps unintentionally) the traditional conception of immense, repeating cycles of civilization, Claude's bizarrely elongated figures adding a visionary strangeness to the scene. The notion of the "indestructible delicacy of nature" also occurs in Ezra Pound's *A Guide To Kulchur*, which I didn't read until several years after having written the poem.

[On Reading *A Treatise...*] the italicized phrase is from Piers Plowman, in which the dancing leaves of the linden are associated with the Incarnation (and thus that sacred knowledge, inseparable from innocence and love, which is at the antipodes of the myopic and as it were pharisaical pedantry typical of modern, profane scholarship).

[Opening The Mouth] Basavanna (1106-1167) was a South Indian devotional poet, "lord of the meeting rivers" being his name for the god Shiva; I encountered his work in A.K. Ramanujan's volume of medieval religious lyrics or *vacanas* (literally "sayings, things said"), *Speaking of Siva* (Penguin Classics, 1973). Internet rumours of the approach of the mythical planet Nibiru were rife in the heady days of 2011, drunk on Mayan prophecies and millenarian dread, and (one assumes) the inspiration for Lars von Trier's film *Melancholia*.

[Dusk: An Antique Song] a version of Heine's unrhymed poem Gotterdammerung, the "twilight of the gods", done in the summer of 2013 and printed in the TLS that autumn (since when it has been slightly revised). If its darkness seems excessive, the least that can be said is that it conforms to reality and the position we occupy in the great cycle of the ages spoken of – with remarkable consistency – by numerous cultures (namely the closing stage of the Iron Age, Kali Yuga, or Age of the Wolf, a time of unbridled rapaciousness and deceit, philosophical materialism, the apotheosis of vice, and ultimately the invisible jail of a wholly mechanized society – a servile, infantilized world in which "everything that has come to predominate… is the exact antithesis of any traditional type of civilization"). It also owes something to the work of the Swiss-German psychologist and psychoanalyst Arno Gruen, and John Lamb Lash's discussion of pre-Christian creation myths in his book *Not In His Image: Gnostic Vision, Sacred Ecology and the Future of Belief* (Chelsea Green Publishing, 2006).

[Minoan] lines suggested by certain vases in the British Museum.

[Reading The Book Of Hills And Seas] T'ao Ch'ien (365-427) was the foremost poet-recluse of the Taoist revival of the third and fourth centuries AD; "reading the book of hills and seas" is the title given to this poem by Arthur Waley in his *One Hundred & Seventy Chinese Poems* (Constable & Co Ltd, 1918).

[Two Zen Poems] the poems are by P'ang Yun (740-808) and Dongshan Liangjie (807-869), two Zen adepts of the T'ang Dynasty. Thusness or *tathatā*, a central concept in both Mahayana and Zen Buddhism, has been described as "reality itself, the real nature of all phenomena, eternal, unchanging, without falsity" (in J.C. Cleary's *Zen Dawn: Early Zen Texts From Tun Huang*), "the non-dual and supremely blissful nature of reality as seen by the enlightened mind" (in Frithjof Schuon's *Treasures of Buddhism*), and "the ultimate essence of every state, object or phenomenon… the quality of that which is perceived, insofar as it is directly and evidentially perceived, as a subject of pure experience, of simplicity, of impersonal transparency" (in Julius Evola's *The Doctrine of Awakening*); it is, Evola adds, "a term as difficult to translate as it is to express the state of rarefied illumination from which it takes its sense".

[Cubist Painting] this poem has its roots in an essay I wrote for Modern Painters in my late twenties, originally titled *The Birth of Painting Out Of The Spirit of Music*, which included a novel interpretation of cubist dismantlings as not so much rational as Dionysian in nature.

[Black & White] the great religious scholar and philosopher of religion Frithjof Schuon has observed that, from an esoteric rather than strictly orthodox (or exoteric) standpoint, "the relationship 'Heaven-hell' corresponds by metaphysical necessity to what is expressed in the Far Eastern symbolism of the *yin-yang*, in which the black portion includes a white point and the white portion a black point; if, then, there are compensations in Gehenna because nothing in existence can be absolute and the Divine Mercy penetrates everywhere, there must also be in Paradise, not indeed sufferings, but shadows bearing an inverse testimony to the same principle of compensation and signifying that Paradise is not God..." (*Understanding Islam: A New Translation with Selected Letters*, World Wisdom 2011).

[Potsherds] these are indebted to G.S. Conway and Richard Stoneman's *Pindar: The Odes and Selected Fragments* (Everyman, 1997), and a handful of liberty cap mushrooms found on a Dartmoor tor; it could therefore be said in all seriousness, as Stoneman writes of Pindar's dithyrambs, that they are "in the Phrygian mode". According to Pindar, one initiated into the Mysteries could die without fear, "for he knows the end of life and he knows its god-sent beginning".

[And The Matter Of The Hour...] the title and first line are from, respectively, chapters 16/*The Bee* and 34/*Sheba* of the Koran, the former in the excellent version of A.J. Arberry (*The Koran Interpreted*, OUP, 1964); "the Friend" is one of the names by which Islamic mystics, or Sufis, refer to God (of the day's proclaiming, Schuon writes that, for the true Muslim, "the world is an immense book filled with 'signs' (*āyāt*) or symbols – elements of beauty – which speak to our understanding and are addressed to 'those who understand'. The world is made up of forms, and they are as it were the fragments of a celestial music that has become frozen; knowledge or sanctity dissolves our frozen state and liberates the inner melody").

[Iron Age] Cf. Purgatorio XXII, 70-71. "The (great) age begins anew, justice returns"; lines spoken by the Roman poet Statius, who is paraphrasing – and, of course, translating – Virgil's fourth Eclogue, in which Virgil prophesies the death of the serpent, the freeing of mankind from its yoke of fraud and fear, and the arising of a new solar race.